T0407426

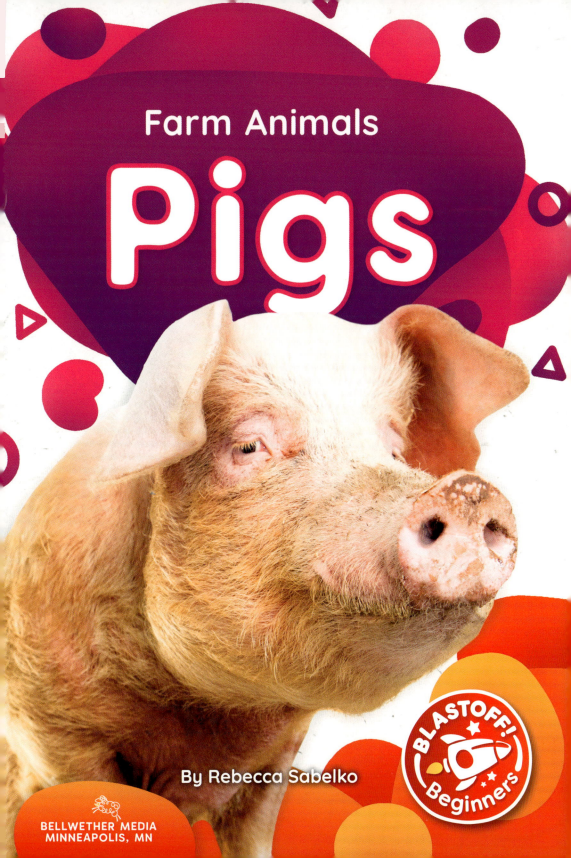

Farm Animals
Pigs

By Rebecca Sabelko

BELLWETHER MEDIA
MINNEAPOLIS, MN

BLASTOFF!
Beginners

Blastoff! Beginners are developed by literacy experts and educators to meet the needs of early readers. These engaging informational texts support young children as they begin reading about their world. Through simple language and high frequency words paired with crisp, colorful photos, Blastoff! Beginners launch young readers into the universe of independent reading.

Blastoff! Universe

Reading Level — Grade K

Grades 1-3

Grade 4

Sight Words in This Book 🔍

and	eat	look	this
are	for	many	to
at	have	on	too
be	in	the	with
big	is	their	
can	it	they	

This edition first published in 2024 by Bellwether Media, Inc.

No part of this publication may be reproduced in whole or in part without written permission of the publisher. For information regarding permission, write to Bellwether Media, Inc., Attention: Permissions Department, 6012 Blue Circle Drive, Minnetonka, MN 55343.

Library of Congress Cataloging-in-Publication Data

Names: Sabelko, Rebecca, author.
Title: Pigs / by Rebecca Sabelko.
Description: Minneapolis, MN : Bellwether Media, 2024. | Series: Blastoff! Beginners: Farm Animals | Includes bibliographical references and index. | Audience: Ages 4-7 | Audience: Grades K-1
Identifiers: LCCN 2023039742 (print) | LCCN 2023039743 (ebook) | ISBN 9798886877632 (library binding) | ISBN 9798886879513 (paperback) | ISBN 9798886878578 (ebook)
Subjects: LCSH: Swine--Juvenile literature.
Classification: LCC SF395.5 .S23 2024 (print) | LCC SF395.5 (ebook) | DDC 636.4--dc23/eng/20230825
LC record available at https://lccn.loc.gov/2023039742
LC ebook record available at https://lccn.loc.gov/2023039743

Editor: Elizabeth Neuenfeldt   Designer: Laura Sowers

Printed in the United States of America, North Mankato, MN.

Table of Contents

Muddy Pig!

The pig rolls in the mud. Look at the muddy pig!

mud

What Are Pigs?

Pigs are
farm animals.
They can
grow big!

Pigs have round bodies. They can be many colors.

Pigs have **snouts**.
Their ears
are pointed.

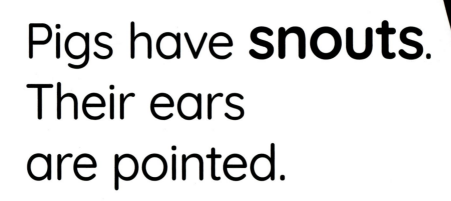

ears

snout

11

Pigs walk on **split hooves**. Many pigs have curly tails!

curly tail

split hooves

Life on the Farm

Pigs live in barns. They keep cool in mud.

barn

They dig with
their snouts.
They dig for bugs.

Farmers give pigs food, too. Pigs eat **feed**.

farmer

feed

bugs

feed

19

This pig
is hungry.
Listen to its oinks
and **squeals**!

Pig Facts

Parts of a Pig

pointed ears

snout

curly tail

split hooves

Life on the Farm

roll in mud

dig with snout

eat bugs and feed

Glossary

feed

food for
farm animals

snouts

the noses
of pigs

split hooves

hard foot
coverings that
have two parts

squeals

the loud noises pigs
make when they
are hungry

To Learn More

ON THE WEB

FACTSURFER

Factsurfer.com gives you a safe, fun way to find more information.

1. Go to www.factsurfer.com.

2. Enter "pigs" into the search box and click 🔍.

3. Select your book cover to see a list of related content.

Index